TRUE
CONFESSIONS

Owning Up to the Secret
Everybody Knows

Philip Yancey

TRUE
CONFESSIONS

Owning Up to the Secret
Everybody Knows

WORD PUBLISHING

Word (UK) Ltd
Milton Keynes, England

WORD BOOKS AUSTRALIA
Heathmont, Victoria, Australia
SUNDAY SCHOOL CENTRE WHOLESALE
Salt River, South Africa
ALBY COMMERCIAL ENTERPRISES PTE LTD
Scotts Road, Singapore
CONCORDE DISTRIBUTORS LTD
Havelock North, New Zealand
CROSS (HK) CO
Hong Kong
PRAISE INC
Quezon City, Philippines

TRUE CONFESSIONS

Copyright © 1987 by Philip Yancey.

First published in the USA by Servant Publications.

First UK Edition 1987.

ISBN 0–85009–137–3 (Australia 1–80258–035–9)

Reproduced, printed and bound in Great Britain for Word (UK) Ltd., by Cox & Wyman Ltd., Reading.

PART ONE

DOES IT REALLY MATTER?

"All day long, and all the days of our life, we are sliding, slipping, falling away—as if God were, to our present consciousness, a smooth inclined plane on which there is no resting."—C.S. Lewis

"I ain't got to, but I can't help it."
—William Faulkner

Sin. The very word has a slithery, reptilian sound to it. For me, the word summons up overtones from the past, when heavy-breathing Southern revivalists would stretch it out in full two-syllable fury. "Siiiiii-yun," they would shout, and raise their fists in defiance against the satanic force that lay in wait for each of us, that lay in wait inside us.

I trembled as a child when I heard about sin and the horrors of its punishment. Subconsciously, my images of God were forming as I listened to those revivalists. God was no Father to me, for I had no image of father to draw on—mine died of polio just after my first birthday. God was more like an authority figure I knew about: a school principal, perhaps, or a teacher. Yes, like one teacher especially. My notion of God resembled the armorplated German matron who inspired fear in the hearts of any first-grader daring to whisper or throw spitballs in her domain. Except God was far larger and stricter, the strictest teacher imaginable.

Martin Luther grew up haunted by a stained-glass window from his boyhood church, a window depicting Christ as a stern King with a raised sword. The sword appeared to Luther exactly like a rod. To my child's mind also, God loomed as the great Enforcer who brought swift and terrible punishment to all who misbehaved. Church members fanned those fears when they told me that my earthly father, now in heaven, was looking down on me to help spy out my hidden sins.

A Vanishing Concept

Now, looking back, my early, oppressive encounters with the word sin seem to belong to someone else who lived on another planet. I rarely come across the word these days in Christian books or magazines, rarely hear it railed against from the pulpit, never hear it on network television. Fear of sin, the dominant force of my childhood, as well as that of many others', has nearly disappeared from view.

Ever since Freud, the idea of behavior as a series of independent moral acts has given way to a much fuzzier notion of behavior as the random expression of the vast subconscious. Partly as a result, the concept of sin is in grave danger of extinction in our culture at large. Not so long ago, George Bernard Shaw called the doctrine of original sin the only empirically verifiable Christian doctrine. But now I doubt whether a single one of the residents of my street would even recognize the term original sin. ("I dunno—maybe some kinky new fad?")

Today, we hear about "the health problems associated with promiscuous sex," or "the problem of illegitimate births" or "the social problems caused by income disparity," but we never hear the word sin. Try dropping "sin" into a conversation on these topics, and you'll see what I mean.

We thus find ourselves in the schizophrenic position of ignoring the most obvious fact about human behavior, the fact of sin. Our psychologists and sociologists avoid the word, as do many of our preachers. So do many ordinary Christians. I suspect if a true prophet from God came in judgment against the sins of our modern culture, he would be greeted first with incredulous laughter, then scorn, then violent opposition. (Curiously, the exact same responses greeted most of the Old Testament prophets.)

As I reflect on my own pilgrimage of faith, I find that it has mirrored the schizophrenia of a larger culture. Sometimes I am dominated by sin-consciousness, sometimes I rebel vigorously against it, but most often I avoid it completely. Yet always I have been plagued by a nagging, underlying sense that I must somehow come to terms with this word that shows up on so many pages of the Bible.

Sin as an abstract idea teaches nothing. Sinners themselves teach much, and perhaps for that reason the Bible expresses in story form most of what it says about sin. And to learn about my own sin, I had to begin by tracing its progress in my life. I had to identify my sin—not just a stray sin here or there, but patterns of sin that keep breaking out. Here are a few sins from my long list.

Deceit. I am ashamed to admit it, but I struggle against a consistent pattern of deceit. Earlier, justifying my deceit as a creative way to oppose "the system," I would engage in such shenanigans as mailing all utility bill payments without postage stamps (causing the utility companies to pay postage, until the Postal Service wised up and stopped delivering such mail) and subscribing to record clubs in order to tape-record the records before sending them back for a refund. Over time, my conscience stricken, I cut out such practices, but I still recognize deep within me a temptation to rely on deceit as a survival tactic when I feel trapped.

Permanent Discontent. You may not find this one on any biblical list of sins, but the root attitude affects me in many sinful ways. Years of working as an editor gave me an editor's personality which is never satisfied. I always want to strike out words, rearrange sentences, crumple up whole first drafts. Such dyspepsia serves a worthwhile purpose in editing, but not in the rest of life. I find myself editing my wife's behavior, and my friends'. I constantly yearn for what I cannot have and cannot be. Mainly, I make myself nearly impervious to that spirit the Bible calls joy.

Hypocrisy. All Christians fight this sin to some degree (there I go again, rationalizing), but writers perhaps more than most. A Christian leader writes a stirring call to civil disobedience. A Nebraska pastor reads it, defies the law in defense of his private school, and lands in jail. How does the Christian leader feel? I write about leprosy patients in India, and about the extraordinary humility and sacrifice of missionaries I have visited there— but I write from the comfort of an air-conditioned office, with the strains of classical music filling the room. How do I live with that? How should I?

Greed. Do you know of any other ministry that has a one-to-one relationship between ministry and income? Authors have such an arrangement. Each person I reach through a book means more money in my pocket. Need I detail the dangers of mixed motives that can result?

Egotism. Again, a most embarrassing admission I would much prefer to leave off my list of sins. But I dare not. Like every other author and speaker, I begin with the rather audacious assumption that I have a viewpoint worth listening to. If I did not believe that, I would not go through the painful process of writing. The danger of pride rides with every thought, every sentence, every word.

You will note that my list of sins excludes many overt ones, such as child abuse, drunkenness, adultery, and cruelty to animals. I am not tempted toward those sins, and that fact offers my first clue into the nature of sin: It strikes at the point of greatest vulnerability.

I spend my days secluded in an office, away from people, susceptible to an introvert's self-absorption. The sins of discontent, egotism, and greed are internal sins. They grow like mold in dark, moist corners of the mind and psyche, nourished by slight rejections, mild paranoia, and loneliness—the precise occupational hazards of every writer.

A brash public figure such as quarterback Jim McMahon or comedienne Joan Rivers will face a different set of temptations. And those who depend for a living on the successful preening of their bodies will likely fall at different points; adultery constantly tempts them, as Hollywood divorce rates easily prove. Similarly, while a poor man struggles with envy, a rich man battles greed.

We who battle internal sins can easily think our sins somehow more respectable than more blatant sins such as adultery and drunkenness. The moment we entertain such thoughts, we fall into an even deeper hole of self-righteousness. I have attended meetings of Alcoholics Anonymous and have never met a recovering alcoholic who denied his or her own sinfulness; but I have met many Christians who find it difficult to confess their own sins. I know such Christians well, for I am one. Malcolm Muggeridge expressed the danger this way:

It is precisely when you consider the best in man that you see there is in each of us a hard core of pride or self-centeredness which corrupts our best achievements and blights our best experiences. It comes out in all sorts of ways— in the jealousy which spoils our friendships, in the vanity we feel when we have done something pretty good, in the easy conversion of love into lust, in the meanness which makes us depreciate the efforts of other people, in the distortion of our own judgement by our own self-interest, in our fondness for flattery and our resentment of blame, in our self-assertive profession of fine ideals which we never begin to practice.

(Ah, I see that I have a compatriot in my list of sins, a fellow author no less.)

We can work up ire against the decay of our society—witness the furor over abortion and violence and pornography and other external sins—but unless we also come to terms with our own private sins, we will have missed the message of the gospel. If you ever doubt that, simply turn to the Sermon on the Mount, in which Jesus painted with one brush lust and adultery, hatred and murder.

A Shift in Outlook

In my childhood, thinking about sin terrified me. In adolescence it repulsed me. Yet now I find myself thinking about sin often, and fruitfully. What caused the change in perspective?

I now recognize that the faith I learned in childhood fixated on sin, stopping short of grace. Only after I experienced firsthand the loving grace of God could I begin to think healthily about sin. I had a guide in learning about grace, a gentle old Scottish Presbyterian minister named George MacDonald. He died in 1858, but he left behind a collection of sermons that have taught me about grace. (Many, edited by Rolland Hein for a modern audience, are found in the books *Life Essential* and *Creation in Christ*.)

George MacDonald preached the gospel of grace so strongly that one of his sons protested, "It all seems too good to be true!" MacDonald replied, "Nay, it is just so good it must be true!" As I immersed myself in the writings of that godly man, many of the calluses that had grown thick against the harsh fundamentalism of my childhood began to soften and fall away. The first to fall was my image of God as a cruel and heartless teacher.

I had viewed God as a cranky old codger who concocted an arbitrary list of rules for the express purpose of making sure everyone would be punished for breaking one or two of them. The rules made no sense in themselves, I thought, especially the 613 Old Testament laws.

George MacDonald showed me another way of looking at law. It was not a new insight, and yet it penetrated me with gradual emotional force until it changed the whole way I viewed God and rules. The key is this: *The rules were not given for God's sake—just so he would have an excuse for punishment—but rather they were given for our sakes.* I suppose I had paid lip service to that truth, but emotionally I was still reacting to my childhood image of God as stern taskmaster.

Every parent knows the difference between rules designed primarily for the benefit of the parent (Don't talk while I'm on the telephone! Clean up your room—your grandmother's coming) and those designed for the benefit of the child (Wear a hat—it's below freezing! But don't skate on the pond yet). The law, even the Old Testament law, primarily fell into the latter category. In Israel, God selected a race of people as "a kingdom of priests, a holy nation" to demonstrate his own holiness. Yet at the same time God, as creator and designer of the human race, knew that human society would work best without adultery, without murder, without lying, without idolatry.

I began to look at the Ten Commandments in this light. They

emerged as the skeleton of a society designed primarily for the benefit of the people themselves. Each negative command could be turned around and stated positively. At its core, each commandment protects something of great value to the human race. Consider a few examples of the commandments restated:

I, the creator, am giving you myself. You will need no worthless images of wood or stone, for you can have me, the Lord of the Universe.

I am giving you my name, and you can be called by my name. Treat it as your sacred possession, and do not defile its meaning by using it in vain.

I have made human life sacred and eternal, stamping my likeness on every child born. Protect and value what I have created. Cause it to live, not die.

I am giving you marriage, and the mystery of love and intimacy between one man and one woman. Preserve it against dilution through adultery.

I do not read Hebrew, but those who do tell me that the familiar English forms "Thou shalt not," and "Thou shalt" may be misleading. In English, the verb "shall" conveys both imperative "You shall obey!" and future ("I shall come Tuesday"). The Hebrew in the Ten Commandments is closer to the future form. God is giving a description of what a holy people will look like.

The nation failed, of course, by breaking the covenant. Then Jesus came with a new covenant based on forgiveness and grace. The apostle Paul, reflecting on that Old Testament history, called it a "schoolmaster to bring us to Christ." "But now," he wrote, "we are discharged from the law, dead to that which held us captive, so that we serve not under the old written code but in the new life of the Spirit" (Rom 7:6).

A Health Expert

For a long time I resisted any thought of God as an authority figure; the harsh images from my childhood had scarred me too deeply. But lately I have been thinking of other images, realizing that in many areas of life I gladly submit to authority. When I encounter a problem with my computer software, I frantically dial a toll-free number and then scrupulously follow the orders of the expert on the other end of the line. When I want to master a new sport, say, downhill skiing, I pay for expensive lessons. And when I am sick, I go to a doctor.

Perhaps that last image of a doctor is the most instructive in thinking about God and sin. What a doctor does for me physically—guides me toward health—God does for me spiritually. I am learning to view sins not as an arbitrary list of rules drawn up by a cranky teacher, but rather as a list of dangerous carcinogens that must be avoided at all costs.

Once I saw in a medical textbook side by side photographs of two sets of lungs. The lungs on the left were a brilliant glossy pink, so shiny and smoothly textured they could have been taken from a newborn. In stark contrast, the lungs next to them looked as if they had been used to clean a chimney. Black sediment coated them, clogging all the delicate membranes designed to capture oxygen molecules. The photo caption explained that the lungs on the left had been removed during the autopsy of a Wyoming farmer; those on the right came from a resident of a factory town who had chain-smoked all his life.

I cannot comprehend how any doctor who has seen such lungs side by side could ever smoke again. And I remind myself of that image when I think about sin. What those impurities do to a person's lungs, sin does to the spiritual life. It retards growth, ravages health, chokes off the supply of new life.

I think back to the sins I have mentioned. What effect do they have on my own spiritual health?

Deceit. What would happen if I ignored warning signs and consistently yielded to promptings toward deceit? No one—not my neighbors, not my wife—could fully trust me. I would become a sad and lonely recluse, isolated by my own duplicity.

Permanent Discontent. I have already said what this tendency produces: an instinctive resistance to joy. It also blocks out gratitude, the emotion doctors judge most nourishing to health. Surely I suffer to the degree that I allow this sin to spread unchecked.

Hypocrisy. Think of the worst hypocrite you know. Do I want to end up like that? Could anyone suggest that a person is better off for hypocrisy, that personal growth is encouraged and not stunted by this sin?

Greed. I know well what greed does to me and my work. When I write, it changes the questions I ask from *Is this thought true? Does it have value?* to *Will it sell?*

Egotism. I battle it even at this moment. Should I really risk exposure in a booklet about sin? Should I write about my spiritual disciplines instead? Or will the strokes I get for honesty outweigh the criticism from those who question my spiritual maturity?

Each of my sins, those I have mentioned and those secret ones I would not dare mention, represent a grave danger to my spiritual health. If I give in to any one of them as a consistent pattern, I will suffer grave loss. My spirit will shrivel and atrophy, just like the lung tissue of the chain-smoker.

The more I see my sins in this light, the more I see beyond the harshness of God's punishments. I find myself gazing into the grieving eyes of a parent whose children are destroying themselves. He responds to our sins both with punishment and forgiveness, which may seem opposites. But, paradoxically, each has exactly the same purpose: to break the stranglehold of sin and make wholeness possible. He offers healing; we choose the cancer.

I confess that it has taken me many years to learn to trust God.

The catalog of sins and the type of authority I encountered as a child proved untrustworthy. But through fits and starts of rebellion, apathy, and occasional obedience, I have learned that God himself can be trusted. I can trust him with my health, and I can trust him with my sins. He welcomes me. As Jesus said, applying the doctor image to himself, "It is not the healthy who need a doctor, but the sick. I have not come to call the righteous, but sinners to repentance."

At times, of course, I do not trust. Sometime today, sometime tomorrow, I will recreate the original rebellion of Eden and act by my standards and my desires, not God's. God cannot overlook such behavior; it must be accounted for, as it was with Adam and Eve. But in that reckoning he aims not to destroy but to heal. No surgeon who wills the health of a patient can effect it without some pain.

The wounded surgeon plies the
steel
That questions the distempered
part;
Beneath the bleeding hands we
feel
The sharp compassion of the
healer's art
Resolving the enigma of the fever
chart.
—T.S. Eliot, *The Four Quartets*

PART TWO

THE SIN CYCLE

Americans who read the newspapers in the early 1970's woke up each morning to some exciting bit of news about sin. The Watergate affair—complete with wiretapping, burglary, bribes, obstruction of justice, firing of prosecutors, denials—unraveled in public, in full view. Every juicy morsel uncovered by nosy reporters was trumpeted in front page headlines for all to see. Eventually, the scandal brought down the President of the United States.

I have said that the Bible teaches us about sin mainly through stories, and its most complete story of sin also involves a national leader, one whose crimes easily overshadow any that were dreamed of during Richard Nixon's darkest moods. The biblical sin began as a moment of simple, everyday lust. It ended in adultery and murder, and cost the lives of hundreds of soldiers. And the villain was arguably the greatest leader in the history of Israel: King David.

The Bible records the sin in all its seamy details, and from it we can learn a lesson about the complete cycle of sin. So far, I've focused on my growing awareness of sin and the reasons I need to pay attention to it. But awareness of a problem does not lead automatically to a cure. An act of sin sets into motion an entire cycle of spiritual disease.

I have identified five stages in the sin cycle which we must move through on the way toward spiritual health. We can easily bog down in any one of the stages; the point is to keep moving forward.

1. Sin. Many people think of sins somewhat like parking tickets. In Chicago, my home city, one single parking ticket matters little. You can ignore it and never get into trouble. Once you get ten, however, you start receiving threatening letters and your name goes into a computer file. If you get stopped for a traffic violation, the police officer will know about your unpaid tickets. And if you accumulate twenty-five tickets, you become a scofflaw. One day you'll walk outside and find your car immobilized, with an ugly steel contraption called a "Denver boot" clamped onto your front wheel. The only way to get the boot removed is to appear in court and pay all your fines.

Similarly, it's common to view individual sins as nuisances that will cause problems only if you accumulate too many. A few niggling little sins may not matter, but eventually you will reach a crisis point and have to face the consequences. The Bible, however, has a far different perspective on sin, as King David's story demonstrates. The Bible views sins more as cancer cells. One or two here and there do make a difference—often the difference between life and death. Cancer cells grow, multiply, and take over, and they may ultimately require major surgery.

You can read David's story (2 Sam 11-20) as an account of the spread of a moral cancer. After the lust for Bathsheba came the adultery, then the cover-up lies, and then the outright murder. But the effect of sin did not stop there. As a result of the whole sordid process, David seemed to lose his grip on his family. One son raped his half-sister. Another son seethed for two years and then committed a murder of revenge. Eventually that same son launched an armed revolt against

David and nearly brought down the kingdom. The later troubles of Israel all traced back to the early sins of King David.

The same pattern, on a different scale, appeared in Watergate: a petty crime, a bungled cover-up, and then a web of deceit and intrigue that finally led to national crisis. And the same pattern can appear in my life or your life: a seemingly harmless white lie or act of lust can lead to terrible consequences. That's why the Bible takes each individual sin so seriously.

2. Guilt. Some psychologists accuse Christians of fostering unhealthy guilt complexes and suggest we would all be better off if we could learn to overcome our feelings of guilt. Their patients may indeed have harmful obsessions with guilt, but many of those unhealthy guilty feelings come from confusing false guilt with true guilt.

False guilt occurs when a person

punishes himself or herself for not measuring up to somebody else's standards: a parent's standards, perhaps, or the church's, or society's. True guilt occurs when a person does not measure up to God's standards.

H.L. Mencken's caricature of a Puritan ("a person with a haunting fear that someone, somewhere is happy") hints at how far the church or society can stray from God's own standards of right and wrong. Jesus Christ himself was criticized by the "Puritans" of his day. The parties he attended had too much wine and feasting, they said, and, besides, he hung around unsavory characters. But Jesus did not experience false guilt from not measuring up to someone else's standards; instead he rebuked the Pharisees for making such unctuous judgments.

There is a healthy place for true guilt, however, and true guilt follows sin as naturally as pain follows injury. When we feel a twinge of conscience, we should first ask whether we've done something deserving true guilt. In other words, have we committed sin? If the answer is yes—as it was in David's case—then we dare not avoid or repress that guilt. Like pain, it warns us of something that endangers our health.

Guilt is not a state to cultivate, like a mood you slip into for a few days. It is directional, first pointing backward to the sin and then pointing forward to repentance. A feeling of guilt may indeed be a sign of God's presence; the most mature Christians are the first to sense any disruption in their communication with God. But they immediately advance from the state of feeling guilty to the next stage: repentance. David understood the process. He sinned grievously and experienced deep guilt when the prophet Nathan confronted him. But he did not wallow in that guilt. He went on to the next stage in the sin cycle.

3. Repentance. After his sin, David recorded his thoughts and emotions during the act of repentance, a record that has come down to us as a permanent legacy in Psalm 51. Many thousands of Jews and Christians have made that psalm their own prayer in response to true guilt.

The poetry of Psalm 51 is so familiar and majestic that we can easily lose sight of its context. Although a public psalm, prayed by the people of Israel, it confesses a horrible private sin committed by the king. Reflect again on the rough American counterpart in Watergate, especially Richard Nixon's response. In his lengthy interviews with David Frost, for example, Nixon never admitted guilt. He would use words like "errors of judgment" and "mistakes," but he never bluntly confessed, "I was wrong. I'm sorry."

In front of television cameras, Nixon responded precisely like most of us do when caught in wrongdoing: We rationalize, explain away, justify ourselves, grudgingly acknowledge error. Nixon's squirming denials were hardly unusual; rather, they revealed under bright lights that the President is just like everyone else. And that is what makes David's approach so extraordinary. He, the king, turned his confession into a public document, a national song. His open confession of failure was unique among all leaders of his day.

To David, restoring a right relationship with God was far more important than maintaining his reputation as a ruler. "Against you, you only, have I sinned and done what is evil in your sight," he prayed, even though his sin had affected many people. He understood that the object of repentance was to bridge the gulf between the sinner and God.

C.S. Lewis said this about repentance: "It is not something God demands of you before He will take you back and which He could let you off if He chose; it is simply a description of what going back is like." For a model of repentance, simply read and reflect on Psalm 51. It has endured for centuries as a remarkable description of a person going back to God. Then ask yourself: Does my response to guilt more resemble David's attitude or Richard Nixon's?

4. Punishment. it would be unfair to hold up David's story as a model of the sin cycle without mentioning the aspect of punishment. He, the anointed ruler of God's people, had failed God miserably and deserved punishment. The prophet Nathan announced that calamity would come out of David's own household,

and 2 Samuel chronicles exactly
how that calamity worked itself out.
The punishment came not through
miraculous intervention by God but
through the normal process of sin
eating away inside the royal
household. Ultimately, Nathan's
prophecy came true: the king's own
son took over Jerusalem and lay
with David's wives in broad daylight.
The cancer had run its course.

The Bible records some instances
of God's direct intervention in
punishment, especially in the period
of time when the Israelites were
wandering in the desert. But more
often the punishment flows
naturally as a result of the sin. Get
drunk enough and your liver will
bear the punishment. Live a life of
debauchery, and you may end up
with venereal disease. Tell lies, and
you'll find yourself isolated and
untrusted. If you flout God's rules,
you risk bringing down punishment
on yourself, whether it take the

form of physical harm, fractured relationships, or a spiritual void.

5. Forgiveness. David offers one of the best and one of the worst examples of forgiveness in the Bible. After his own sin, he followed the cycle of guilt, repentance, punishment, and forgiveness in textbook fashion. Psalm 51 plumbs his sorrow and remorse at committing the sin, and God answered his plea. David got a pure heart, and his joy was restored. His reconciliation with God became a centerpiece in the Old Testament, a beautiful picture of the forgiveness to come through Jesus. David also endured the punishment of Absalom's rebellion, but he rebounded, regained the throne, and served as one of Israel's greatest kings.

"A man after God's own heart," David was called, though he had committed adultery and murder.

His life defines the boundaries of forgiveness. In a final touch, God even accepted the second offspring of his liaison with Bathsheba, the boy Solomon, as the next favored king of Israel. Spiritual giants like David—and also Peter, the denier of Christ, and Paul, the persecuter of Christians—demonstrate that God can forgive any sin and restore any sinner to full acceptance and usefulness.

Yet David, a textbook example of the sin cycle, badly botched the process within his own family. He proved inept at punishing his sons. When his son Amnon raped his half-sister, David fumed but took no action, perhaps out of insecurity about his moral authority after the affair with Bathsheba. And when Absalom took revenge against Amnon into his own hands, David's only punishment was to shut Absalom out of the house.

Even when Absalom lived in the

capital city of Jerusalem, David refused to see him face to face. He couldn't bring himself to punish him, and he couldn't bring himself to forgive him. Desperate, Absalom tried arson as an attempt to get his father's attention. He demanded either a murder trial or reconciliation. Finally, after five years David kissed and made up, but he never officially dealt with the crimes that had been committed. His pride wounded beyond repair, Absalom organized a violent revolt against his father. David had proved much better at receiving forgiveness than giving it.

In one of his short stories, Ernest Hemingway refers to a Madrid anecdote about a father who decides to reconcile with his son. Years before, the boy had run away to Madrid, and the father, like King David, had cut off all contact with his son. The father takes out this ad in a Madrid newspaper: "Paco, meet me at Hotel Montana noon Tuesday. All is forgiven. Papa." Paco is a common name in Spain, and when the father went to the square, he found eight hundred young men named Paco waiting for their fathers.

We were born sinners, and we sin each day. But we were also born hungering for forgiveness. Almost by instinct we yearn for that clean, fresh feeling of restoration, of being made new. A desperate desire for it lives in each one of us. And it is the state God promises if we turn to him. He gave his Son in order to make it possible.

"I ain't got to, but I can't help it," said one of William Faulkner's characters about sin. None of us can help it. But when we do sin, we face choices on how to respond. We can yield to the temptation and sin for all we're worth, risking our self-destruction in the process. We can wallow in remorse and live under a constant cloud of guilt. Or we can advance from guilt to repentance and then forgiveness, and take God at his word.

This is how we shall know that we are children of the truth and can reassure ourselves in the sight of God, even if our own conscience makes us feel guilty. For God is greater than our conscience, and he knows everything. And if, dear friends of mine, our conscience no longer accuses us, we may have the utmost confidence in God's presence. (1 Jn 3:19-22, J.B. Phillips version)

Other Titles in the Christian Essentials Series

God in Our Midst
Seeking and Receiving Ongoing Revival
James I. Packer

J.I. Packer believes that God's people urgently need revival. He tells us what renewal is and then explains how to get there.

To Live or Die
Facing Decisions at the End of Life
C. Everett Koop, M.D.

Dr. Koop explores the complex issues surrounding death and dying and offers a Christian approach to making decisions, for oneself and others.

Women: the Challenge and the Call
An Agenda for Christian Women in Today's World
Dee Jepsen

It is time for both men and women to understand the vital importance of a woman's contributions in the church and in society. Dee Jepsen calls women to assert themselves against the forces that threaten to destroy family life— widespread pornography, the erosion of respect for human life, and the pursuit of selfishness.

Word (UK) Ltd.
9 Holdom Avenue,
Bletchley, Milton Keynes